Montenegrin Cookbook
Small Collection of Recipes from a Small Country

Lukas Prochazka

Copyright © 2019 Lukas Prochazka
All rights reserved.
ISBN: 9781079068481

License Note

No part of this book is permitted to be reproduce in any form or by any means This book is subject to the copyright laws of the Czech Republic. All recipes in this book are written only for informative purpose. All readers should be advised to follow the instruction at their own risk.

For more cookbooks please visit
www.amazon.com/author/prochazkacook

CONTENTS

About Montenegro 7

Soups

Pea soup 10
Čorba od crnjaka, Onion soup 11
Čorba od koprive, Nettle soup 12
Green bean soup 13
Jagnjeća supa, Lamb soup 14
Kokošija supa, Chicken soup 15
Otkos čorba, Hay soup 16
Pasulj 17
Shepherd cream soup with mushrooms 18
Teleća supa, Beef soup 19

Main Courses

Balšića tava 22
Black risotto 23
Boiled lamb with rice 24
Carp fillet 25
Cevapi 26
Ćufte, Meatballs 27
Đuveč 28
Goulash 29
Japraci 30
Kačamak 31
Kuvana krtola 32
Lamb in milk 33
Moussaka 35
Pilaf 37
Pljeskavica 38
Punjena paprika 39
Ražnjići 40
Sarma 41
Sataraš 42
Stuffed cabbage with lamb Chops 43

Desserts

Apple strudel 46
Baklava 47
Crepes 49
Keks Torta, Biscuit Cake 50
Krempita 51
Krofne 52

Lenja Pita, Lazy Cake 53
Padobranci 54
Tulumba 55

Volume Conversion 56
Weights of Common Ingredients 57
Temperature Conversion 58
Length Conversion 59

About Montenegro

Montenegro is a country rich in tradition and culture, natural resources and good hosts. In this the beautiful, diverse country, one thing is certain – you will eat well. Whether you are on the coast by commitment to some of the seafood dishes or inside try some of the traditional dishes, your impression will certainly be positive. Montenegrin cuisine is formed under the influence of many traditions and cultures, most of the Mediterranean and Ottoman.

One of the favorite local dishes is raštan, a dish made from a cabbage family vegetable with white potatoes and spices. Montenegrins love and cooked dishes and soups are implicit in every lunch. The Montenegrin thick soups are made from noodles, vegetables or potato. An interesting variation involves the use of nettle. Almost all thick soups include the use of fresh meat, so that they are rich and nutritious. One of the specialties that is worth trying is the lamb in milk.

As for the bread, the older generation of Montenegrins prefer the corn bread; the usual "white" loaves, which are being called "European bread" by the older generation, is popular among the young people.

Sweets are worth a separate topic. The delicious crepes - a large pancake filled with jam, chocolate, cream or "krofne" – small. You can have them in any café together with a cup of strong coffee, hot chocolate or fruit cocktail. Also one can try the "sweet ice", its title speaks for itself.

Don't forget about the spirits of Montenegro. Vranac is the great wine which has almost the ruby colour and has a noble fruity hint. Krstac, the dry white wine with a great flavor, is also popular. The grape rakia is a grape vodka with alc. 50 vol., but it has a great aftertaste and is easier to drink than the usual vodka. Rakia gets its unique aroma because of the Montenegrin "vranac" grape breed. The premium grade of grape rakia is kruna, which has a balanced taste, easy to drink, especially if you have prosciutto, cheese and jerked beef as refreshments. There's one more type of rakia in Montenegro – lozovaca, plum rakia, and apricot rakia - kajsievaca.

Soups

Pea soup

Yields: 2

Ingredients

1 cup yellow split peas
4 tbsp olive oil
1 small onion, chopped
3 cloves garlic
1 small carrot, cut in 1/2 inch cubes
2 medium potatoes
1/2 cup celery, diced
1/2 cup green cabbage, cut in 1/2 inch pieces
1/2 cup white wine
2 cups vegetable stock
2/3 cup unseeded prunes
2 bay leaves
1 tsp cayenne pepper
1 tbsp white wine vinegar
1/2 tbsp honey
Sea salt and freshly ground pepper to taste

Directions

1. In a pot, bring 1 quart water to a boil. Add the split peas and cook for 15 to 20 minutes or until tender. Drain and set aside.
2. In a large pan, heat the oil over medium heat. Saute onion, garlic, carrots, potato, celery and cabbage until tender. Add white wine and vegetable stock and cook for seven to 10 minutes. Then add the remaining ingredients.
3. Adjust seasoning to taste. Serve.

Čorba od crnjaka, Onion soup

Yields: 6

Ingredients

Olive oil
3 lbs red onions, peeled, sliced 1/8-inch thick
Salt and pepper
1 cup dry red wine
2 bay leaves
1 small bunch thyme, tied with string
8 garlic cloves, roughly chopped
2 tbsps brandy (optional)
6 slices day-old bread, lightly toasted
6 oz grated Gruyère
1 tsp chopped thyme
1 tbsp chopped sage

Dierctions

1. Set 2 large, wide skillets over medium-high heat. When pans are hot, add 1 tablespoon oil and a large handful of sliced onions to each pan. Season onions with salt and pepper, then sauté, stirring occasionally, until they are a ruddy dark brown, about 10 minutes
2. Transfer onions to soup pot and return pans to stove. Pour 1/2 cup water into each pan to deglaze it, scraping with a wooden spoon to dissolve any brown bits. Pour deglazing liquid into soup pot.
3. Wipe pans clean with paper towel and begin again with more oil and sliced onions. Continue until all onions are used. Don't crowd pans or onions won't brown sufficiently.
4. Place soup pot over high heat. Add wine, bay leaves, thyme bunch and garlic. Simmer rapidly for 5 minutes, then add 8 cups water and return to boil. Turn heat down to maintain a gentle simmer.
5. Add 2 teaspoons salt. Cook for 45 minutes. Skim off any surface fat, taste and adjust seasoning. (May be prepared to this point up to 2 days in advance.)
6. To serve, add brandy to soup, if using, and simmer 5 minutes. Remove the thyme. Make the cheese toasts: Heat broiler. Place toasted bread on baking sheet. Mix grated cheese with chopped thyme and sage, along with a generous amount of pepper. Heap about 1 ounce of cheese mixture on each toast. Broil until cheese bubbles and browns slightly.
7. Ladle soup into wide bowls and top with toast.

Čorba od koprive, Nettle soup

Yields: 4

Ingredients

1 tbsp olive oil
1 onion, chopped
1 carrot, diced
1 leek, washed and finely sliced
1 large potato, thinly sliced
1l vegetable stock
1 lb stinging or dead nettles, washed, leaves picked
1 1/2 oz butter, diced
1 1/2 oz double cream

Directions

1. Heat the oil in a large saucepan over a medium heat. Add the onion, carrot, leek and potato, and cook for 10 mins until the vegetables start to soften.
2. Add the stock and cook for a further 10-15 mins until the potato is soft.
3. Add the nettle leaves, simmer for 1 min to wilt, then blend the soup. Season to taste, then stir in the butter and cream.
4. Serve the soup drizzled with extra oil and scattered with dead nettle flowers, if you have them.

Green bean soup

Yields: 6

Ingredients

2 lbs fresh green beans
1 clove garlic, minced
1 sprig fresh parsley
1 pinch salt
2 slices bacon
3 tbsps all-purpose flour
1 onion, chopped
1 cup sour cream

Directions

1. In a large pot over medium heat, combine green beans, garlic, parsley, salt and water to cover and cook until beans are tender.
2. Fry bacon until crisp, set aside. Add onion and flour to bacon grease, stirring until smooth and brown. Add some water from the beans, stirring slowly and constantly to prevent lumps.
3. Cook to thicken a bit, then add it to the bean soup and bring to a boil. Stir crisp bacon, sour cream and vinegar.

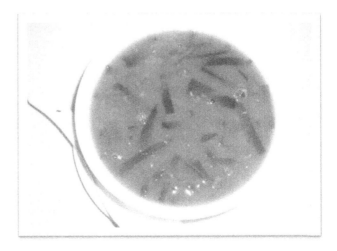

Jagnjeća supa, Lamb soup

Yields: 6

Ingredients

6 veal cutlets
1 lb lamb ribs
4 potatoes (large)
1/2 lb flat green beans
1 garlic head (unpeeled)
1 onion (large)
3-4 bell peppers (large)
1 1/2 tsp seasoned salt (or Vegeta)
1 tsp pepper
Oil
2 tbsp butter

Directions

1. Preheat oven to 480°F.
2. Season meat with seasoned salt. Warm some oil in a pan over high heat. Once the oil is very hot, brown meat on each side (approximately 2-3 minutes per side). Remove meat from the pan, and pour remaining oil into a clay pot, or glass bakeware.
3. Cut onion into eight pieces, and place in the pot together with the garlic head. Layer meat around and on top. Deseed peppers, peel potatoes and cut all into quarters lengthwise. Layer on top of meat, and add beans. Cover tightly with lid, or foil (you can make 2-3 holes in foil with a toothpick). Bake for 30 minutes.
4. Lower heat to 390°F and bake another 30 minutes. Uncover and add butter on top. Serve in clay or ceramic bowls.

Kokošija supa, Chicken soup

Yields: 6

Ingredients

1 1/2 lb chicken
2 oz chicken livers
1/2 oz chicken hearts
1/2 oz chicken stomachs
1/2 lb carrots
4 oz tomatoes
1/4 lb onions
4 oz parsley roots
2 oz celery root
1/3 oz
Salt
Black pepper

Directions

1. Put cold water in a pot (appropriate large pot). If you want better soup put chicken in cold water, if you want better chicken meat put it in hot water.
2. Rind carrots, onion, parsley, celery and put all other ingredients into water. Boil and after it boils reduce heat and cook for 3 to 4 hours.
3. Filter the soup into separate pot.
4. If you want, put into strained soup carrots, chicken meat (or liver, stomach, or hearts) and add noodles or whatever you like in soup and serve.

Otkos čorba, Hay soup

Yields: 4

Ingredients

1 onion
1 carrots
1/4 lb celery
3 oz pearl barley
1 tbsp butter
1 handful hay
1 1/2l chicken broth
2 tbsps vegetable oil
5 oz whipping cream
2 tbsps whipped whipping cream
Salt
Freshly ground Pepper

Directions

1. Peel and dice onion, carrot and celery. Heat oil in a pan and sauté hay. Add stock, bring to a boil, remove from heat and leave for 30 minutes. Strain through a sieve.
2. Heat butter in a pan. Brown vegetables and barley, stirring constantly. Add broth and simmer for about 1 hour.
3. Add cream and puree soup in a food processor. Season with salt and pepper. Serve with a dollop of whipped cream.

Pasulj

Yields: 6

Ingredients

1/2 lb dried white beans
3/4 lb dried pork ribs
2 onions, chopped
1 large carrot, sliced
1 bay leaf
1 fresh chilli, optional
2 tsp ground red paprika
1 parsley root, chopped
1 tsp pepper or to taste
1 tsp Vegeta (or salt) or to taste
3 tbsp oil
2 tbsp flour
3-4 cloves garlic, minced
2 tsp parsley

Directions

1. Place the beans in a soup pot, cover them with the water. Bring it to a boil. Pour off the first water.
2. Add approx 3 litres of fresh water to the pot of simmered beans, dried Pork Ribs, onions, carrot, bay leaf, parsley root, pepper and 1 chilli paprika (optional). Bring to boil and reduce heat to cook gently over lower heat for 1-1.5 hours, until the beans are soft
3. In a separate saucepan, heat the oil, add 1 chopped onion. Simmer for 5 minutes. Add 2 tbsp of flour and stir it for about 3 min. Quickly stir in the fresh minced garlic and ground red paprika. Mix to a thin paste.
4. Add the saucepan content to the pot of cooked beans. Simmer for a further 5-10 minutes, until the soup is thick and rich.
5. Before serving sprinkle 2 tsp of fresh parsley on top

Shepherd cream soup with mushrooms

Yields: 6

Ingredients

4 tablespoons butter
1 tablespoon oil
2 onions diced
4 cloves garlic minced
1 1/2 lb fresh brown mushrooms sliced
4 tsp chopped thyme divided
1/2 cup Marsala wine
6 tbsp all-purpose flour
4 cups low sodium chicken broth or stock
1-2 tsp salt adjust to taste
1/2-1 tsp black cracked pepper adjust to taste
2 beef bouillon cubes, crumbled
1 cup heavy cream or half and half
Chopped fresh parsley and thyme to serve

Directions

1. Heat butter and oil in a large pot over medium-high heat until melted. Sauté onion for 2 to 3 minutes until softened. Cook garlic until fragrant, about 1 minute.
2. Add mushrooms and 2 teaspoons thyme, cook for 5 minutes. Pour in wine and allow to cook for 3 minutes.
3. Sprinkle mushrooms with flour, mix well and cook for 2 minutes. Add stock, mix again and bring to a boil. Reduce heat to low-medium heat, season with salt, pepper and crumbled bouillon cubes.
4. Cover and allow to simmer for 10-15 minutes, while occasionally stirring, until thickened.
5. Reduce heat to low, stir in cream or half and half. Allow to gently simmer (do not boil). Adjust salt and pepper to your taste.
6. Mix in parsley and remaining thyme. Serve warm.

Teleća supa, Beef soup

Yields: 6

Ingredients

1 lb beef chuck
1 lb beef chuck
2 carrots (medium)
2 celery sticks (or 1 celery root)
2 handfuls of parsley
1 tsp seasoning salt
Pepper to taste
1/2 onion
2 handfuls noodles

Directions

1. Place beef chuck, carrots, celery sticks (root), seasoning salt, pepper, and one handful of parsley into a pot and cover with 64oz of water. Brown the onion on one side by placing it directly on a stove burner for a few minutes, and then transfer into the soup.
2. Bring soup to a boil. Reduce heat and let simmer for 2 hours. Add little bit of water as necessary throughout simmering to replenish water lost by heat.
3. Take the meat and carrot out, cut away from the bone and dice. Set aside.
4. Take out the celery root, onion, and parsley and discard.
5. Strain soup back into a different pot, add beef and carrot back in. Take the remaining, fresh parsley, dice and add to the soup. Add two generous handfuls of noodles. Simmer for another 10 minutes.

Main Courses

Balšića tava

Yields: 6

Ingredients

2 lbs boned veal
4 oz carrots, chopped
4 oz onions, chopped
2 oz butter, melted
1 bayleaf
Salt, to taste
3 eggs
7 oz sour cream
2 1/2 quart whole milk
1/2 bunch of parsley

Directions

1. Cut the veal into about 1 oz chunks, add to a pan along with the vegetables and bayleaf. Cover the contents of the pan with water and season to taste. Bring to a boil, reduce to a simmer, then cook for about 40 minutes, or until tender. Drain the meat then place in a roasting pan and drizzle the melted butter over the top.
2. Transfer to an oven pre-heated to 380°F and roast for about 8 minutes. Meanwhile, form the "royal sauce". Whisk together the eggs, milk and cream. Pour over the meat, until completely covered then return to the oven and cook for 5 minutes more, or until lightly golden.
3. Ladle into bowls, garnish with the parsley and serve.

Black risotto

Yields: 4

Ingredients

3 tbsp extra virgin olive oil
1 onion, peeled and finely chopped
1 garlic clove, crushed and peeled
2 lbs of squid, cleaned (ink sacs reserved) and cut into thin strips
1 tsp squid ink, (optional)
4 oz dry white wine
1 tbsp tomato purée
3 oz unsalted butter
1 lb risotto rice
2oz dry white wine
1 1/ quart fish stock, heated
Fine sea salt
Freshly ground black pepper
2 tbsp of flat-leaf parsley, finely chopped

Directions

1. In a saucepan set over a medium heat, fry the onion in olive oil until soft and translucent. Add the garlic and the squid with the ink diluted in a tablespoon of warm water. Cook until the liquid of the squid has evaporated
2. Increase the heat and add the wine and tomato concentrate. Allow the wine to evaporate, then lower the heat again, cover and let simmer for about 30 minutes, stirring often and checking for doneness – the squid should be very tender. Add a little water if you see it becoming too dry. Once ready, remove from the heat and set aside
3. Melt the butter in a separate, large pan. Add the rice and toast it for a couple of minutes, stirring often, until it looks opaque and smells fragrant. Pour over the wine and allow it to evaporate, then start adding a ladleful of hot stock and, as you see it being absorbed by the rice, add some more
4. Carry on this way, adding stock a little at the time, for about 16–18 minutes, stirring all the while. Halfway through, stir in the black squid sauce. Taste and season accordingly
5. When the rice feels tender but is still al dente and the risotto looks creamy and wet, remove from the heat and add the butter and parsley; stir energetically until fully incorporated
6. Spoon the risotto onto flat serving plates and pat it so that it spreads across the plate. Serve straight away

Boiled lamb with rice

Yields: 5

Ingredients

1 small onion minced
2 tbsp soy sauce
2 tbsp olive oil
3 large eggs
6 scallion
1/4 cup mint (chopped)
2 cloves garlic (minced)
3 cups cooked brown rice
2 cups mixed vegetables
2 cups lamb meat
1 inch fresh ginger minced
1 pinch red pepper flakes

Directions

1. Heat 1 tablespoon of the oil in a well-seasoned wok or large non-stick skillet over medium-high heat. Swirl to coat the pan. Pour in the eggs, swirl the pan so the egg forms a large thin pancake.
2. As soon as the egg has set, turn it out of the pan onto a cutting board. Cool, cut into small pieces.
3. Wipe out the pan with a paper towel and heat the remaining oil over high heat. Add the onion and stir-fry for 1 1/2 minutes.
4. Add the garlic, red pepper flakes, and ginger, stir-fry for 1 minute more. Add the soy sauce, and rice and stir-fry for 2 to 3 minutes. Add the lamb meat, mixed vegetables , and reserved egg, cook, stirring until heated through, about 2 to 3 minutes.
5. Sprinkle with mint and Serve immediately.

Carp fillet

Yields: 2

Ingredients

1 lb carp fillet
1 red pepper
1 tomato
1 large onion
4-5 garlic cloves
1 chili
Coarse salt
Black pepper, vinegar
Lovage, bay leaf, dill, thyme, parsley

Directions

1. Roast all the vegetables on an open flame or even in the oven. The char you get from the open flame is much better for flavor. Peel the pepper and the tomato, cut in small cubes, slice the garlic, cut the bigger rings of onion.
2. On a griddle pan, place a thin layer of coarse salt. See salt, or even rock salt. Heat until the salt starts to almost smoke.
3. Portion the fish and place on the griddle, skin side down first for about 6-7 minutes. The skin will protect the fish from burning and will be discarded later. Turn the fish and cook for a further 3-4 minutes until done.
4. Leave to cool for a couple of minutes, peel the skin and remove most of the salt from the fish. The remaining salt will be just enough to season the brine.
5. Add some water to a pan and bring to boil. Lower the fire, add all the veg, the chili (fresh or dried), the bay leaf, thyme, lovage, season with some black pepper.
6. Add a couple of spoons of vinegar. To taste. Turn the fire off and add the fish pieces, cover and let it steep for 10 minutes in the brine, it will flavor from all the vegetables and herbs.
7. Serve hot, preferably with soft golden polenta and sprinkle some fresh parsley over the top just before serving.

Cevapi

Yields: 4

Ingredients

3/4 lb ground beef
3/4 lb ground lamb
3 tbsps finely grated onion
1 tbsp freshly minced garlic
1 1/2 tsps paprika
1 1/2 tsps Kosher salt
1 1/2 tsps freshly ground black pepper
3/4 tsp baking soda

Directions

1. In a medium bowl, mix together beef, lamb, onion, garlic, paprika, salt, pepper, and baking soda by hand until thoroughly combined.
2. Form meat mixture into finger-length sausages 3/4-inch in diameter.
3. Light one chimney full of charcoal. When all the charcoal is lit and covered with gray ash, pour out and spread the coals evenly over entire surface of coal grate. Set cooking grate in place, cover grill and allow to preheat for 5 minutes. Clean and oil the grilling grate.
4. Grill sausages over medium-high direct heat until well browned on all sides and just cooked through, about 8 minutes total. Remove to a serving tray or plates, let rest for 5 minutes, then serve immediately.
5. Serve with comum bread or cooked potatoes and onions.

Ćufte, Meatballs

Yields: 4

Ingredients

1 lb ground beef
1 egg
1/2 cup breadcrumbs
1/4 cup lukewarm water
1 garlic clove, minced
1/4 tsp ground nutmeg
1 tsp chopped fresh parsley
1 tbsp flour
8 oz tomato sauce
1 tsp dried oregano
1 tsp chopped fresh basil
2 tbsp oil
1 small onion, chopped and divided
Salt and pepper to taste

Directions

1. Mix ground beef, half of the onions, garlic, egg, breadcrumbs, nutmeg, parsley, water, salt and pepper in a large bowl by hand until just combined. Roll meatballs to about the size of a golf ball.
2. Roll each into flour to give it a good coating. Heat the oil in a large skillet over medium-high.
3. Fry meatballs until just browned, about 3-4 minutes on each side. Don't worry about the center getting cooked through as you will finish these in the sauce. Remove from the skillet and keep warm.
4. Add 1 tablespoon flour to the skillet and brown until golden but not brown. Add remaining chopped onions and sauté until softened. Add tomato sauce, oregano and basil and bring to a low simmer.
5. Arrange meatballs in the sauce, turning each one over to coat. Cover and simmer gently for 15-20 minutes.
6. Serve with the sauce over spaghetti or other pasta and crusty bread. Sprinkle with chopped parsley for garnish if you want.

Đuveč

Yields: 4

Ingredients

1 cup uncooked rice
2 cups vegetable broth
1/2 cup chopped onion
1/2 cup chopped bell pepper
1 medium carrot chopped
2 cloves garlic minced
2 tomatoes
1/2 cup frozen or fresh peas
1 tsp paprika
1/2 tsp chili powder optional
2 tbsps oil
Salt and pepper to taste
Fresh parsley leaves for garnish

Directions

1. In a medium size pan, heat the oil over medium-high heat. Sauté onion, pepper, and carrot until softened, about 3 minutes.
2. Add garlic and chopped tomatoes then cook for 5 more minutes stirring frequently.
3. Mix in the rice, peas, paprika, and chili powder, if using. If you like it spicy, adjust the amount of chili powder.
4. Next, add broth and bring to a boil. Lower the heat, cover and cook until liquid is absorbed, about 10 to 15 minutes, stirring occasionally.
5. Add salt and pepper to taste. Sprinkle with chopped parsley leaves.

Goulash

Yields: 6

Ingredients

1 tbsp Olive Oil
1 lb Organic Angus Beef /beef for stew, cubed into bite size
1/2 onion medium size
3 garlic cloves minced or sliced
2 carrots shredded or sliced
2 celery ribs, sliced
1 tbsp sweet paprika
1/2 cup tomato sauce
1/2 sp tomato paste
2 cups beef stock low sodium
3 cups pure water
1 dry Bay leaf
1 rosemary sprig
1/2 tsp ground black pepper
Salt to taste
2 lbs Russet potatoes, approximately

Directions

1. In a large pot with a fitted lid, add oil and heat it.
2. Meanwhile, slice/cube beef and sprinkle a generous amount of salt (about a teaspoon), massage it to coat. Add Beef cubes to the pot and brown each cube on all sides (after the oil is heated, turn the temperature to medium).
3. After the beef is browned on each side, add sliced onion, garlic, carrots, and celery. Mix it very well, and sprinkle with sweet paprika. Keep mixing until the vegetables are somewhat cooked halfway, about 4-5 minutes.
4. Pour in Tomato sauce, add tomato paste and liquid (beef stock and water 1 cup at this time). You might want to add more water as it cooks and liquid evaporates.
5. Lastly, add bay leaf, rosemary, ground black pepper and salt to taste. (remember* some tomato sauces are loaded with sodium, so TASTE it before adding more salt).
6. Allow it to boil, cover, turn the heat on medium LOW and let it cook for 2 hours and 20 minutes. Occasionally check, add more water if needed, and stir. If you want it soupier, add more liquid,
7. 30 minutes before you take it off, peel potatoes and cut into large cubes. Add in the soup, cover and let it cook until tender, about 30 minutes.
8. Pull out herbs before serving, and enjoy it.

Japraci

Yields: 4

Ingredients

2 lbs raštan (vegetable with hard green leaves)
1 lb veal
3/4 oz oil
5 oz onions
2 oz rice
Pepper and parsley as needed
1/2 lb dry meat

Directions

1. Separate fresh, good and young leaves of raštan from the stem and remove the thick part of the leaf. Wash in cold water and boil in boiling slated – sour water for a couple of minutes. When the leaves are blanched, take them out and put immediately into cold water so as to preserve their natural colour. Keep in cold water till you use them again.
2. Separate veal neck or shoulder-joint from bones, surplus tough parts and fat and cut in small pieces. Clean onions, wash and chop. Clean and wash rice, and then strain well. If we add dry meat when preparing japraci, it must be cut and put so that one portion contains one piece. Fry on grease chopped onions in an adequate heated vessel. Add chopped meat to onions and fry all together.
3. When onions and meat are fried add the prepared rice and fry all together. Season the mass with a little salt, ground pepper and parsley. Let the prepared stuffing cool. Put the stuffing in leaves and roll it. Boil rolls in pot for 2 hours. Serve with kiselo mlijeko - yogurt

Kačamak

Yields: 4

Ingredients

1 lb corn flour
1 l water
1 small spoon of salt
1 small spoon of fat

Directions

1. Pour 1 l of water into an average deep pan, add 1 small spoon of salt and cook it until the water starts to boil.
2. Into the boiling water slowly pour the corn flour, piece by piece, continuously whisking with a wooden ladle, thus preventing to form unwanted corn flour lumps. Add the salt according to taste during the cooking process
3. After a few minutes of boiling, slow down and weaken the cooking temperature and cook it for about twenty minutes more, continuously whisking the content in a pan, until it gets wanted density. Some people like it more densely, and some like it subtile.
4. Turn off the stove plate switch and leave the cooked hominy on a hot stove plate for about 1/2 an hour more before serving.

Kuvana krtola

Yields: 4

Ingredients

4 large potatoes
8 tbsps yogurt
8 tbsps fresh cheese
1 1/3 teaspoon salt
Dash of freshly ground pepper

Directions

1. Boil or bake the potato until tender (baked is preferable). Peel it and cut it into halves, maintaining the long shape. Arrange them on a plate.
2. Mix the rest of the ingredients and spread them on top of the potato halves. It's done, dig in while it's warm.

Lamb in milk

Yields: 6

Ingredients

1 1/2 lb lamb shoulder cut into 1 1/2 inch pieces
5 tbsps grass-fed butter
2 tbsps pastry flour
1/4 cup arborio (risotto) or any other short grain rice
4 cloves garlic, minced
1/4 cup finely chopped oregano
1/4 cup finely chopped mint
3-4 cups Greek yogurt depending on the size of your baking dish
4 eggs, beaten
Kosher salt and freshly ground black pepper, to taste

Directions

1. Preheat your oven to 350 degrees Fahrenheit.
2. Take a small baking dish and line it with 1 tablespoon of your butter Place your chunks of lamb into the baking dish and season well with salt and pepper. Once the oven is heated bake lamb for 40 minutes.
3. While the lamb is baking in the oven, take a small pot for your rice. Add ½ cup of water to the pot and bring to a boil.
4. Pre-cook your rice for 7 minutes as most of the water soaks up, then take the pot off the heat and set your pre-cooked rice aside
5. Take the baking dish out once the lamb has baked, then drain the liquid that's accumulated in the baking pan. Set your lamb pieces aside.
6. In a small saucepot, melt 3 tablespoons of butter over medium heat
7. Once the butter is nice and heated, add your garlic and oregano and cook for 1 minute
8. As the garlic starts to brown, add a dash of water and 1 tablespoon of your flour in. A thick paste should start to form as you whisk the flour in
9. Once added and thickened, add the accumulated liquid from the baked lamb into the stockpot. Whisk well into the thickened paste
10. Add your last tablespoon into the mixture to thicken it once more. Whisk it well in, then take the stockpot off the heat and let cool for 5 minutes.
11. Once your roux has cooled to slightly above room temperature, add the Greek yogurt and beaten eggs into the saucepot.
12. Fold all the ingredients thoroughly together with one another to get a slightly runny, yellowish sauce.

13. In your baking pan, spread your lamb pieces evenly around.
14. Next, sprinkle the rice over the lamb and into the empty spaces.
15. Then, pour the yogurt sauce over the lamb and rice until the baking dish is fully covered.
16. Finally, cut your last ½ tablespoon of butter into smaller pieces and distribute over the top. Once distributed, place the baking dish into your oven again and bake for 40-45 minutes.
17. Once golden brown, remove from the oven, let cool and sprinkle the fresh mint over top.

Moussaka

Yields: 6

Ingredients

6 eggplants
Vegetable oil
2 lbs beef or lamb mince
2 red onions (chopped)
2 cloves of garlic (chopped)
1 tin chopped tomatoes
2 tbsps tomato puree
1 tsp sugar
1 glass of red wine
Sea salt and freshly ground black pepper
1 bay leaf
Pinch of cinnamon or one cinnamon stick
1/4 cup olive oil
4 cups milk
4 oz butter
4 oz flour
Pinch of nutmeg
2 egg yolks
4 oz Parmigiano-Reggiano or Kefalotyri

Directions

1. To prepare this Greek moussaka recipe, begin by preparing the eggplants. Remove the stalks from the eggplants and cut them into slices, 1 inch thick. Season with salt and place in a colander for about half an hour.
2. Rinse the eggplants with plenty of water and squeeze with your hands, to get rid of the excessive water. Pat them dry and fry in plenty of oil, until nicely colored. Place the fried eggplants on some paper, in order to absorb the oil. (For a lighter version of the traditional Greek moussaka try drizzling the aubergines with some olive oil and bake them for 20 minutes instead of frying them).
3. Prepare the meat sauce for the moussaka. Heat a large pan to medium -high heat and add the olive oil. Stir in the chopped onions and sauté, until softened and slightly colored. Stir in the garlic, tomato puree and the mince breaking it up with a wooden spoon and sauté. Pour in the red wine and wait to evaporate. Add the tinned tomatoes, the sugar, a pinch of cinnamon, 1 bay leaf and a good pinch of salt and pepper. Bring to the boil, turn the heat down and simmer with the lid on for about 30 minutes, until most of the juices have evaporated.

4. Prepare the béchamel sauce for the moussaka. Use a large pan to melt some butter over low-medium heat. Add the flour whisking continuously to make a paste. Add warmed milk in a steady stream; keep whisking in order to prevent your sauce from getting lumpy. If the sauce still needs to thicken, boil over low heat while continuing to stir. Remove the pan from the stove and stir in the egg yolks, salt, pepper, a pinch of nutmeg and the grated cheese. Whisk quickly, in order to prevent the eggs from turning an omelette.
5. Assemble the moussaka. For this moussaka recipe you will need a large baking dish, approx. 15x25 inches). Butter the bottom and sides of the pan and layer the eggplants. Pour in the meat sauce and even out. Add a second layer of eggplants, top with the béchamel sauce and smooth out with a spatula.
6. Sprinkle with grated cheese and bake the musaka in preheated oven at 180-200C for about 60 minutes, until crust turns light golden brown.
7. Serve the Moussaka with a nice refreshing Greek feta salad and enjoy over a glass of wine.

Pilaf

Yields: 4

Ingredients

2 2/3 cup low-sodium chicken broth
1/3 cup unsalted butter
1 tsp kosher sea salt
1/2 tsp garlic powder
1/4 tsp ground black pepper
1/8 tsp paprika
Pinch onion powder
2 tbsps olive oil
1/3 cup vermicelli or orzo
1 cup long-grain white rice
1 tbsp chopped fresh parsley

Directions

1. In a medium saucepan set over medium heat, add the chicken broth, butter, salt, garlic powder, pepper, paprika, and onion powder. Once the mixture starts to simmer, reduce to low heat.
2. In a large skillet set over medium-low heat, add the olive oil. When the oil is hot, add the vermicelli and cook until brown, about 4-6 minutes. Add the rice and cook until it turns bright white, about 5-7 minutes.
3. Pour the warm broth mixture into the skillet, stir to combine. Once the mixture simmers, cover and cook for 15 minutes. Remove the cover, add the parsley, cover and continue cooking for 5 minutes or until all of the broth is absorbed.
4. Serve immediately.

Pljeskavica

Yields: 6

Ingredients

1 lb ground beef
1 lb ground pork
2 tsps salt
1 tsp sweet paprika
1/2 tsp black pepper
1/2 cup sparkling water
2 tbsps olive oil
2 medium onions, finely chopped
Vegetable oil
4 pita bread or somum bread
Ajvar
Kajmak (or other soft cheese)
Onions
Pickles

Directions

1. In a bowl, mix ground beef and pork, salt, sweet paprika, black pepper and sparkling water. Combine with your hands. Brush olive oil on the surface of the meat mixture. It will help us to retain moisture. Cover with plastic wrap and refrigerate for at least few hours or overnight.
2. Add onions to the meat mixture and mix well. Divide to 4 balls and use your hands to pound it to a thin patty. The size should be about 6-7 inches in diameter.
3. Grill or fry your patties for about 3-4 minutes per side or more, if desired. Take bread pockets and assemble your burgers by spreading ajvar and kajmak and adding onions and pickles as desired.

Punjena paprika

Yields: 6

Ingredients

8 white peppers
1 1/2 pound ground beef
1/3 cup rice
1 large potato diced finely
1 small onion diced finely
3 garlic cloves, minced
1 tbsp flat leaf parsley, chopped
1 egg
1 tsp vegeta spice
1 tsp salt
1/2 tsp freshly ground pepper
3 tbsps cooking oil
2 tbsps flour
1 tsp ground paprika
1 tsp salt
1/2 cup tomato purée
4 cups water

Directions

1. Wash and dry the peppers, cut open the top and remove all the seeds and membrane, set aside. Cook the rice halfway about 5 minutes, strain and set aside.
2. In a bowl, mix together the meat, spices, all the vegetables, rice, egg and parsley. Stuff each pepper with the mixture.
3. Heat 3 tablespoons of oil in a large stock pot. Lightly brown the peppers on each side, just a short time, until fragrant. Remove the peppers from the pot and set aside, reserving the oil in the pot.
4. Add 2 tablespoons to the warm oil and stir until smooth. Add the ground paprika and salt, stir for a minute, taking care that it does not burn. Add tomato purée and water, stir and let boil. Add in the peppers, turn the temperature down to medium, cover and simmer for 1 hour.
5. The sauce will reduce and thicken as the peppers cook
6. Serve with a side of mashed potatoes and lots of sauce.

Ražnjići

Yields: 8

Ingredients

1/2 cup red wine vinegar
1/2 cup vegetable oil
1 large sweet onion, chopped
3 tbsps garlic cloves, chopped
2 tbsps fresh parsley, chopped
2 lb pork tenderloin, diced
Salt and pepper

Directions

1. In a gallon-sized resealable bag, mix together red wine vinegar, vegetable oil, onions, garlic and parsley.
2. Add pork to bag and marinate in the fridge for at least 4 hours (8-10 hours for maximum flavor).
3. If using wooden skewers, let soak in water for 30 minutes. Remove pork from marinade and thread onto skewers, packing them tightly. Generously season pork with salt and pepper.
4. Preheat grill to high heat.
5. Grill pork for 3-4 minutes on each side or until pork is cooked thoroughly.

Sarma

Yields: 6

Ingredients

1 large head cabbage
1 lb ground chuck
1/2 lb ground pork
1 cup raw rice
1 package dehydrated onion soup mix
1 jar sauerkraut
6 smoked ribs
1 can tomato sauce
1 can tomato soup

Directions

1. Steam cabbage until outer leaves are limp, then remove leaves. With a paring knife, remove tough ribs from leaves without damaging them. Reserve tougher outer leaves, but don't use for rolling.
2. In a medium bowl, mix together ground chuck, ground pork, rice, and onion soup mix. Adding a little water will make the mixture easier to handle.
3. Heap 2 tablespoons of filling on each cabbage leaf. Fold the bottom of the cabbage leaf up over meat. Then fold sides to the center, and roll away from yourself to encase completely. Repeat until meat filling is gone.
4. Heat oven to 350 F. Discard the cabbage core and coarsely chop any remaining cabbage except the tough outer leaves you have reserved.
5. Spread chopped cabbage on the bottom of a large casserole dish or Dutch oven. Add the sauerkraut. Layer on the cabbage rolls, seam side down.
6. Cut the smoked ribs into pieces if using, otherwise, space the smoked meat of choice between the cabbage rolls. Cover rolls with reserved tough outer leaves.
7. Mix tomato sauce and soup with enough water to make a liquidy consistency. Pour over rolls until mixture is level with rolls, but not over the top.
8. Cover casserole dish and bake 1 hour. Then reduce temperature to 325 F and bake for 2 more hours.
9. Let sit 20 to 30 minutes before serving.

Sataraš

Yields: 2

Ingredients

2 yellow peppers
4 tomatoes
2 onions
A little bit of oil
Seasoning, salt, pepper

Directions

1. Simmer chopped peppers and onions with some oil (sliced into smaller lobules) until browned and tender.
2. Meanwhile peel the tomatoes (we want get rid of the peel), chop it into smaller pieces and add it to the pepper and onion.
3. Stir and season as desired, and simmer until all the liquid has evaporated. Addition of water is not necessary.

Stuffed cabbage with lamb Chops

Yields: 6

Ingredients

4 lbs lamb chops
2 lbs minced lean ground beef
6 lbs White cabbage
2 oz cinnamon powder
2 oz chopped mint leaves
1 oz dry mint leaves
5 oz chopped onions
5 oz ghee
1 lb egyptian rice
3 oz hite pepper
2 oz garlic
1/5 oz cumin
1 oz maggie
1/2 tbsp Salt
3 tbsp olive oil
4 whole lemon
4 cups water

Directions

1. Heat grill pan over high heat until almost smoking, add the lamb chops and sear for about 2 minutes. Flip the chops over and cook for another 3 minutes. Set aside
2. Peel and discard the outer leaves of the cabbage. To separate the leaves, simmer the entire cabbage head in a large pot of boiling water for 5-10 minutes, carefully turning it over to ensure exposure to all of its side-
3. As the leaves loosen, pin down the cabbage inside the pot with one fork, and with another fork slowly peel away the leaves one after the other. Do this slowly and carefully so you don't hurt yourself with boiling water, and to also ensure that leaves are whole and not torn.
4. Place the cabbage leaves in a colander as you peel them. Please note that if you try to peel leaves of a raw cabbage they'll very likely break and tear
5. Once you've separated all leaves, try to roll one or two of them to see if they are soft enough. If not, and if they tear or break, put them back in the boiling water pot and cook them for another 5 minutes

6. Mix the minced meat with cinnamon powder, cumin, ghee, garlic, onion and Egyptian rice. Season with salt to taste. Mix them well and set aside
7. Lay each cabbage leaf separately on a cutting board, cut out the stem if it's too thick. Spread 1 to 2 table spoons of meat stuffing along the edge of the leaf. Roll it slowly and tightly over the meat all the way
8. Place the grilled lamb chops in a wide/deep cooking pot and line up the stuffed rolls carefully on top of the grilled chops one by the other in a compact manner until you've completed a layer which you will garnish with a few chopped cloves of garlic, sliced potatoes and mint leaves
9. Squeeze 4 lemons, mix them with 4 cups of water, ½ to 1 teaspoon of salt (to taste), chopped garlic, maggie and dry mint then add them to the cooking pot. The sauce should cover the rolls and if not, add more water until it does
10. Carefully shake/tilt the cooking pot sideways a few times to ensure the sauce seeps through everywhere. Place a heavy plate inside the pot, on top of the rolls, cover the pot, and turn on the stove on high heat for about 5-10 minutes until they boil, at which time you turn heat to very low and let them simmer slowly for 1 to 1.5 hours (until the cabbage is fully cooked and is no longer crunchy - time may vary, however you should be left with a bit of sauce on the bottom don't let it dry up)
11. Serve hot.

Desserts

Apple strudel

Yields: 6

Ingredients

1 Granny Smith apple, peeled, cored and coarsely shredded
3 Granny Smith apples, peeled, cored and sliced
1 cup brown sugar
1 cup golden raisins
1 sheet frozen puff pastry, thawed
1 egg
1/4 cup milk

Directions

1. Preheat oven to 400F. Line a baking sheet with parchment paper.
2. Place apples in a large bowl. Stir in brown sugar and golden raisins; set aside. Place puff pastry on baking sheet. Roll lightly with a rolling pin.
3. Arrange apple filling down the middle of the pastry lengthwise. Fold the pastry lengthwise around the mixture. Seal edges of pastry by using a bit of water on your fingers, and rubbing the pastry edges together. Whisk egg and milk together, and brush onto top of pastry.
4. Bake in preheated oven for 35 to 40 minutes, or until golden brown.

Baklava

Yields: 6

Ingredients

16 oz phyllo dough (or puff pastry)
1 1/4 cups butter, melted
1 lb walnuts, finely chopped
1 tsp ground cinnamon
1 cup granulated sugar
3/4 cup water
1/2 cup honey
2 tbsps lemon juice

Directions

1. Thaw phyllo dough completely by placing it in the fridge overnight, then letting the package of phyllo sit, unopened, on the counter for 1 hour prior to making your baklava so it can come all the way to room temperature.
2. Butter the bottom and sides of a large rectangular 9x13-inch baking dish. Trim phyllo to fit in the dish, if necessary. I have seen 16 oz. pkgs. of phyllo that come with either 18 large sheets in one roll or 40 smaller sheets in 2 rolls. Either works, so long as you have 16 oz. of phyllo. I just cut the 18 large sheets in half down the middle to fit, giving 36 sheets. The 40 smaller sheets might just need to be trimmed slightly around the edges. Keep trimmed dough covered in a damp cloth so it doesn't dry out.
3. Chop walnuts in a food processor by pulsing 10-12 times until coarsely ground or chop with a knife until very finely chopped. Stir together the walnuts and cinnamon until combined.
4. Prepare the sauce before assembling the baklava so it has plenty of time to cool completely before pouring over the baked phyllo dough.
5. Combine the sugar, water, honey, and lemon juice in a medium saucepan and bring to a boil over medium-high heat, stirring until the sugar dissolves.
6. Reduce heat to medium-low and continue to boil for 4 minutes more without stirring. Remove from heat and cool completely.
7. Heat oven to 325°F.
8. Sprinkle approximately 1/5 of the chopped walnuts and cinnamon (roughly 3/4 cup) in a thin, even layer over the first 10 sheets of phyllo dough.
9. Repeat 4 more times but with 5 sheets of phyllo dough instead of 10, brushing each with between before adding the next sheet and sprinkling with 3/4 cup of the chopped walnut mixture between each layer of 5 sheets of buttered phyllo dough.

10. Finish the baklava with a final, top layer of phyllo dough brushed with butter between the layers using the remaining 6-10 sheets of dough. Brush the top sheet of phyllo dough with butter as well.
11. Carefully slice the baklava into 1 1/2-inch wide strips lengthwise, then slice diagonally to create diamond-shaped baklava. Or just slice squares if you prefer.
12. Bake in the 325°F oven for 1 hour and 15 minutes, until the baklava is golden brown. Remove from oven and immediately drizzle all of the cooled syrup over the baklava.
13. Let the baklava cool completely at room temperature for 4-6 hours without being covered so the baked pastry can soak up all of the syrup. The finished baklava can be store for 1 to 2 weeks at room temperature, covered with just a clean tea towel.

Crepes

Yields: 7

Ingredients

10 oz white flour
2 eggs
1/2 tsp salt
2 cups milk
1 cup water
1 cup oil
10 ounces jam or preserve
Whipped cream

Directions

1. Combine flour, eggs, salt and milk in a larger bowl. Mix the batter with a spatula for a few minutes, then turn on the hand mixer. Continue mixing with the hand mixer, slowly adding water as necessary. Mix until the batter is free of crumbs, and is completely smooth with a consistency of heavy cream.
2. Pour oil into a small bowl. Take a paper towel and dip it in the oil, and then use the paper towel to coat the crepe pan with it. Heat up the pan on the highest until it's really hot.
3. Transfer batter into the pan by using a ladle (fill it up about 2/3s). Watching that the batter doesn't leave the pan, swirl it around until the batter coats the pan bottom evenly. When the crepe has slightly browned on the bottom (about 30 seconds), flip it around to the other side. Place the finished crepe on a plate.
4. Oil the pan with a paper towel. Heat the pan again, then repeat the process until you are out of batter.
5. Fill crepes with jam and roll them to tight rolls. Garnish with whipped cream. Serve.

Keks Torta, Biscuit Cake

Yields: 10

Ingredients

10 large egg whites
2 1/2 cups sugar
10 1/2 oz walnuts. ground
2 tbsps bread crumbs
10 oz chocolate, chopped
4 sticks butter
5 large egg whites
1 cup sugar

Directions

1. Whip egg whites until stiff. Slowly add sugar and again whip to stiff peaks. Mix walnuts with breadcrumbs and gently fold into egg whites until well incorporated.
2. Divide batter evenly among prepared loaf pans and bake about 7 to 12 minutes or until the center springs back when lightly pressed and edges are just beginning to color. Remove from oven and cool in pan 3 minutes.
3. Run a knife around the edge of the sponge cake to loosen it. Carefully invert onto a cooling rack and peel off the parchment paper. Let cool completely. When cool, split each sponge cake in half horizontally so you have 8 layers.
4. Melt chocolate in a microwave and set aside to cool to room temperature. In a large bowl, beat butter on low for 2 minutes, then on medium for 3 minutes and finally on high for 5 minutes.
5. Place egg whites and sugar in a double boiler over medium heat. Transfer to a mixing bowl and whip on high until stiff peaks form.
6. Fold the melted chocolate into the whipped butter, then gently fold in the egg whites until all traces of white are gone. Refrigerate until ready to use.
7. Place one layer of walnut sponge on a serving tray and spread on a layer of chocolate filling. Repeat until all eight layers are stacked on top of each other.
8. Frost the top and sides of the torte with the remaining chocolate filling. If desired, garnish with a sprinkle of chopped walnuts but this is not necessary.

Krempita

Yields: 6

Ingredients

2 sheets puff pastry
6 large egg yolks
6 tbsps sugar
2 tbsps instant flour
1 1/2 cups milk
2 packages unflavored gelatin
2 tbsps vanilla sugar
1 quart heavy cream
Powdered sugar

Directions

1. Heat oven to 400 F. Roll out each piece of puff pastry slightly to blend the seam lines. Without cutting all the way through, lightly score each pastry sheet into 9 sections. Sandwich each puff pastry sheet between two pieces of parchment paper and two cooling racks. This will keep the pastry flat but still flaky.
2. Bake 15 minutes, remove top rack and top sheet of parchment paper. Replace rack and continue to bake until golden and crispy throughout, about 15 more minutes. Cool completely.
3. Whip the egg yolks and sugar until thick and lemon colored. Add the instant flour and milk, mixing well. Transfer to the top of a double boiler. Cook, stirring constantly until custard thickens slightly.
4. Remove from heat. Dissolve gelatin completely in 1/2 cup cold water. Stir into hot custard until completely dissolved.
5. Cool the custard in an ice bath, stirring occasionally. If, for some reason, the custard has lumps (from being cooked at too high a temperature or undissolved gelatin), strain it through a sieve.
6. When the custard is cool and very thick but not yet set, fold in the sweetened whipped cream. Layer over 1 sheet of baked puff pastry and top with a second sheet. Refrigerate at least 1 hour before serving. For easier slicing, use a damp serrated knife. Cut into rectangles. Dust with confectioners' sugar.

Krofne

Yields: 6

Ingredients

1 package active dry yeast
2 tbsps sugar
1 tsp salt
1/4 cup warm milk
1/4 cup warm water
1 lb flour, and some for dusting
1/2 cup milk
1/2 cup water
1/4 canola oil
3 eggs
Canola oil
Raspberry jam
Icing sugar

Directions

1. Combine ¼ cup of warm water and ¼ cup of warm milk with sugar, salt and yeast. Stir well and set aside for 10 minutes until mixture starts to bubble.
2. Knead the dough using sifted flour, yeast mixture, milk, water, canola oil and beaten eggs. When the dough is mixed well, remove it to the oiled bowl and cover with cloth or plastic wrap. Wait to rise for 1 hour until doubled in size.
3. Then punch the dough one more time and wait for 30 minutes to rise again
4. Spread the dough on work surface dusted with flour. Using rolling pin stretch the dough and when it's 1/3 inch thick use a 2 inch diameter circle cutter to make rounds. Repeat the same process with the dough leftovers. Make a hollow on the top side of each dough round using your finger - that's where you will put jam filling.
5. Heat the canola oil in a small pan. Fry doughnuts in medium hot oil for 2-3 minutes each side, till they get nice brown colour.
6. When doughnuts are fried remove them to the paper towel. Then, fill each with the jam. Sprinkle doughnuts with icing sugar.

Lenja Pita, Lazy Cake

Yields: 4

Ingredients

1/2 lb margarine
1/4 lb lard
1 lb sugar
4 eggs
2 cups of milk
1 1/2 lbs flour
1 sachet of baking powder
Vanilla sugar
2 lbs sour apples

Directions

1. Stir together margarine and lard, add 10 tablespoons of sugar and 4 egg yolks and continue stirring well.
2. Add 2 cups of milk, flour mixed with a baking powder and vanilla sugar. Knead the dough.
3. Put more than half of dough in greased baking pan, then well beat 4 egg whites with 6 tablespoons of sugar and pour over the dough in the pan. Add sour grated apples to all of that.
4. Spread the rest of the dough to form the crust that fit pan shape and place it over filling.
5. Place the pie into the medium heated oven and bake until the crust is golden brown.
6. Sprinkle powder sugar over warm pie.

Padobranci

Yields: 6

Ingredients

4 egg whites
1/2 lb icing sugar
1/2 lb ground walnuts
2 tsp lemon juice or vinegar
1 tbsp corn flour (or fine biscuit crumbs)
Cream
4 oz butter, soft
4 oz icing sugar
2 egg yolks
2 oz chocolate, melted

Directions

1. Beat egg whites until soft peak forms; add sugar, spoon by spoon. Beat until sugar dissolved and egg whites thick. Fold in lemon juice, corn flour, walnuts and corn flour.
2. Preheat oven to 300F line biscuit tins with baking pape.
3. Pipe or spoon meringue into little circles, with some space between them. Bake / dry for 1 hour; switch oven off and let macaroons cool inside ajared oven.
4. For cream; beat butter, sugar and yolks until thick and fluffy. Add melted chocolate, mix well.
5. When macaroons are cooled, place some of cream on one and top with another-one.
6. Keep in a cool, dry spot.

Tulumba

Yields: 6

Ingredients

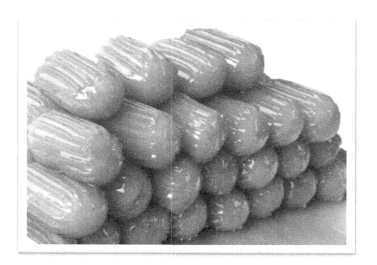

3 cups sugar
3 1/2 cups water
1 tbsp lemon juice
2 tbsps butter
2 tbsps sugar
2 cups water
2 1/2 cups flour
3 large eggs
3 tbsps semolina
2 tbsps cornstarch
3 cups vegetable oil
Ground nuts

Directions

1. In a saucepan, stir 3 cups sugar and 3 1/2 cups water together. Bring the mixture to a boil and stir until the sugar is dissolved.
2. Reduce the heat and let the syrup simmer gently for about 15 minutes. Add the lemon juice and simmer for 1 minute longer. Turn off the heat and let it cool.
3. In a saucepan, add butter, 2 tablespoons sugar, and 2 cups water. Turn on the heat and stir continuously until the butter is melted.
4. Stir in the flour using a wooden spoon until a loose dough forms.
5. When the dough begins to collect around the spoon, remove the pan from the heat and set it aside to cool.
6. Break one egg at a time into the dough and stir them in with the wooden spoon.
7. Add the semolina and cornstarch, combining well with the wooden spoon.
8. Transfer batter to a pastry bag fitted with a star tip.
9. Pour about 3 inches of vegetable oil into a deep frying pan and heat to 350 F, checking it with a thermometer.
10. Once the oil is hot, squeeze out small lines of dough directly into the hot oil. Use a strainer or spoon to turn the pieces over and around so they brown evenly.
11. When the tulumba are evenly browned, remove them from the oil and drain on paper towels.
12. Add them to the cool syrup and let them soak it up.
13. Arrange the syrupy sweets on a serving plate and pour some extra syrup over the top. You can garnish the tulumba with ground nuts if you wish.

Volume Conversion

Customary Quantity	Metric Equivalent
1 teaspoon	5 ml
1 tablespoon	15ml
1/8 cup	30 ml
1/4 cup	60 ml
1/3 cup	80 ml
1/2 cup	120 ml
2/3 cup	160 ml
3/4 cup	180 ml
1 cup	240 ml
1 1/2 cups	360 ml
2 cups	480 ml
3 cups	720 ml
4 cups	960 ml

Weights of Common Ingredients

Ingredient	1 cup	1/2 cup	2 Tbs
Flour	120 g	70 g	15 g
Sugar	200 g	100 g	25 g
Rice	190 g	100 g	24 g
Macaroni	140 g	70 g	17 g
Butter	240 g	120 g	30 g
Chopped Nuts	150 g	75 g	20 g
Bread Crumbs	150 g	75 g	20 g
Grated Cheese	90 g	45 g	11 g

Temperature Conversion

Fahrenheit	Celsius
250	120
275	140
300	150
325	160
c350	180
375	190
400	200
425	220
450	203

Length Conversion

Inch	cm
0,125	0,32
0,25	0,63
0,5	1,27
1	2,54
2	5,08
5	12,7

Thank you for investing time and money to read this book!

I hope you have enjoyed this book as much as possible and that you have learnt something new and interesting. If you have enjoyed this book, please take a few minutes to write a review summarizing your thoughts and opinion about this book.

If you are interested in other books of mine check out my official amazon author's profile:

www.amazon.com/author/prochazkacook

Thanks for buying this book and have best of luck.

Sincerely,

Lukas Prochazka

Learn more about world cuisines

If you are interested in other cookbook you should consider checking out these honorable mentions.

Traditional Spanish cuisine is down-to-earth, uncomplicated food that is based on the ingredients available locally or the crops grown regionally. Learn the basics of Spanish cuisine, including popular Spanish cooking ingredients and common methods for preparing Spanish cuisine.

Austria was once a great empire. It was a melting pot of dozens of cultures standing under one flag and under one leader. In its capital city of Vienna, the best of each part combined to make one of the best cuisines of all the world.

When talking about European cuisines, there are big players like France or Italy that steal the spotlight. Most of foreigners are unfamiliar with the most of Eastern and Southern Europe. Yet that's the place where the most interesting and exotic European tastes manifest.

Made in United States
North Haven, CT
21 December 2022

29892199R00037